CARMELO ANTHONY

BY PAUL HOBLIN

Published by ABDO Publishing Company, PO Box 398166, Minneapolis, MN 55439. Copyright © 2012 by Abdo Consulting Group, Inc. International copyrights reserved in all countries. No part of this book may be reproduced in any form without written permission from the publisher. SportsZone™ is a trademark and logo of ABDO Publishing Company.

Printed in the United States of America,
North Mankato, Minnesota
092011
012012

Editor: Chrös McDougall
Copy Editor: Anna Comstock
Series Design: Craig Hinton
Cover and Interior Production: Kazuko Collins

Photo Credits: John Raoux/AP Images, cover, 1; Bill Kostroun/AP Images, 4; Mitchell Layton/NBAE/Getty Images, 7; Jeff Zelevansky/AP Images, 9; Kevin Rivoli/AP Images, 10, 15; Brett Wilhelm/NCAA Photos/AP Images, 13; Ed Reinke/AP Images, 17; Kevork Djansezian/AP Images, 18; Douglas C. Pizac/AP Images, 21; Mark J. Terrill/AP Images, 23; Garrett Elwood/NBAE/Getty Images, 24; Casey Rodgers/AP Images for InStyle, 27; Darron Cummings/AP Images, 29

Library of Congress Cataloging-in-Publication Data

Hoblin, Paul.
  Carmelo Anthony : superstar scorer / by Paul Hoblin.
    p. cm. — (Playmakers)
  Includes bibliographical references and index.
  ISBN 978-1-61783-289-5
  1. Anthony, Carmelo, 1984—Juvenile literature. 2. Basketball players—United States—Biography—Juvenile literature. I. Title.
  GV884.A58H63 2012
  796.323092—dc23
  [B]
                              2011038206

TABLE OF CONTENTS

Carmelo Anthony

CHAPTER 1

SMILES AND SLAM DUNKS

It is hardly surprising that Carmelo Anthony loves basketball. After all, he is a National Basketball Association (NBA) star. But as a kid, he did not even have a real hoop to shoot at. Instead, Carmelo had a square crate that was attached to a building. He and his friends pretended the crate was a hoop. They still loved to play, though. Even though they eventually got a real hoop, the crate is still there today!

New York Knicks star Carmelo Anthony did not even have a real basketball hoop when he was young.

Carmelo was born in Brooklyn, New York. That is part of New York City. Carmelo and his mom later moved to Baltimore, Maryland. He was eight years old when they moved. Carmelo now has a tattoo that says "West Baltimore." He never wants to forget where he grew up.

Carmelo's nickname is Melo. His dad's nickname was Curley. However, Melo never got to hear anyone use his dad's nickname. Curley died when Carmelo was still a baby.

The people in West Baltimore have never forgotten Carmelo either. They remember how he was always playing basketball. He was already a gym rat in middle school. Friends would find him in the gym working on his game whenever he had free time. Basketball helped Carmelo stay out of trouble. Of course, it was also a way to have fun.

People from Carmelo's old neighborhood remember his smile as well. He always seemed to be smiling and having a good time. That has not changed since he became an NBA star.

Carmelo continues to give back to the community through the Carmelo Anthony Youth Development Center in Baltimore.

Carmelo always loved basketball. But he was not always a star. Carmelo went to Towson Catholic High School. He was cut from the varsity team as a freshman. Not making the team was tough for Carmelo. But he did not lose his love for the game.

Carmelo kept practicing. He also kept growing. In fact, he grew five inches taller before his sophomore season. He made the varsity team that year. And he was the team's star player!

He was even better the next year. In fact, Carmelo was named the Baltimore City and Council Player of the Year. He still had one more year of high school. But several college coaches were already interested in having Carmelo play for their teams. He decided to play for Syracuse University in upstate New York after high school.

Carmelo played a lot of basketball during the summer before his senior year. He had the chance to play with and against some of the best high school basketball players in the nation. Two of these players were Amare Stoudemire and LeBron James. They both went on to become NBA stars as well. Carmelo and LeBron quickly became good friends.

Carmelo still had one more year of high school. This turned out to be a problem. He loved basketball, but he did not love school. His grades were not very good. He had to improve them in order to play in college. Carmelo and his mother decided that Oak Hill Academy in Virginia might be a better fit for him.

Carmelo was really homesick in Virginia. But he also knew that the school was a good choice. It was known for both its academics and its basketball. Before Carmelo, 14 former

Carmelo played in the 2002 McDonald's All-American Game. It is a high school All-Star game.

Oak Hill players had gone to the NBA. Many of his Oak Hill teammates also were being recruited to play basketball in college. Carmelo was still the team's best player, though. Many thought he was the best high school player in the nation.

Carmelo also did better in school. Both his grades and his test scores improved enough for him to go to college. Fans of the Syracuse basketball team would soon be glad they did.

CHAPTER 2

SWISHING IN SYRACUSE

Carmelo Anthony had been born in New York. But he had spent most of his life in Maryland and Virginia. So, he needed some time to adjust when he arrived at Syracuse in 2002. The hardest part to get used to was the cold weather. He was not used to upstate New York's freezing winters.

Anthony was ready to play basketball, though. He scored 21 points in the first half of his first college

Anthony averaged more than 22 points per game as a freshman at Syracuse.

game. The game was played in Madison Square Garden in New York City. That is where the NBA's New York Knicks play their home games. Anthony hoped to one day play in that arena as an NBA star himself. Little did he know he would actually star for the Knicks.

For now, Anthony was focused on his college team. Many expected the Syracuse Orangemen to struggle during Anthony's freshman year. They were a young team. Most people thought the players needed more experience. But Anthony and his teammates showed their talent. They quickly became one of the best teams in the nation.

Anthony and his teammates showed they were for real during a late-season game against the Notre Dame Fighting Irish. Both teams were among the top teams in the Big East Conference. The winner would move into first place.

The sports teams at Syracuse were named the Orangemen when Anthony played there. However, the school changed the nickname to the Orange before the 2004–05 season.

Anthony led Syracuse in points and rebounds per game as a freshman.

Notre Dame started the game strong. The Irish held a lead into the second half. Then Anthony scored 18 of his 26 total points. That led Syracuse to victory.

Syracuse fans soon started yelling, "One more year! One more year!" They knew that Anthony was already good enough to play in the NBA. But they hoped he would stay on their team for at least one more season.

Of course, the season was not over yet. Syracuse had qualified for the national championship tournament!

The tournament had 65 of the best teams in the country. Teams that won moved on to the next round while the losers went home. The last team standing was the national champion.

The Orangemen won their first game of the tournament. They were favored to beat Oklahoma State in the second round. But Anthony and his teammates soon found themselves losing by 17 points. Anthony was playing his worst game of the season. He finally started making some shots, though. And he and his teammates rallied back to win the game.

They won their next two games after that, too. The Orangemen had made it to the Final Four. This meant they were one of only four teams left. It also meant they had to play a really good team—the Texas Longhorns. They were one of the favorites to win the whole tournament. The Longhorns' best player was T. J. Ford. He had recently been named the nation's best player. Syracuse, meanwhile, had already done better than most people expected.

Anthony was named an All-American during the 2002–03 season. Only the very best players receive that honor.

Ford played well against Syracuse. But Anthony played better. He had one of his best games of the season as the Orangemen won 95–84. He played so well that he could not help but smile after he made some of his shots.

Few expected Syracuse to be a top team that season. Now the Orangemen were just one game away from the national title. Only the Kansas Jayhawks stood in their way.

The Syracuse players again found themselves as the underdogs. Kansas had several veteran players. Many of them had played together for years. Two Kansas players would go onto the NBA. Their coach, Roy Williams, was considered one of the best ever. The Orangemen also had a respected coach in Jim Boeheim. But Anthony was the team's best player. And he was only a freshman!

Anthony scored 33 points against the Texas Longhorns in the 2003 Final Four. He also set a record for most points by a freshman in the national championship tournament. Afterward, Anthony was named the Most Outstanding Player of the tournament.

The game was close. However, Anthony and his teammates found a way to win. Anthony had led Syracuse in scoring in 23 of its 34 games so far that season. With 20 points, he again led the Orangemen in the championship game. Anthony was all smiles as he congratulated his teammates and his coach.

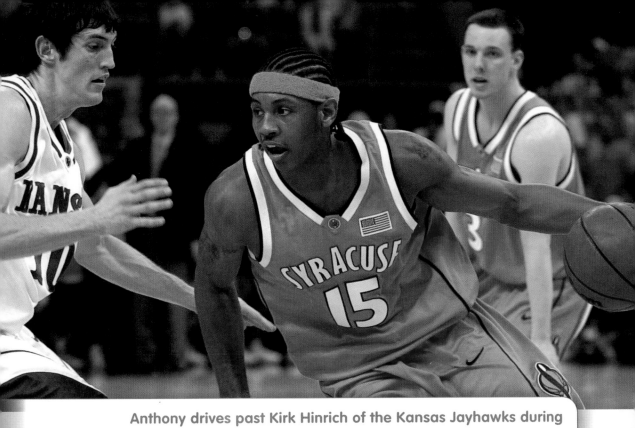

Anthony drives past Kirk Hinrich of the Kansas Jayhawks during the 2003 national championship game.

And Anthony had more to smile about than just the national championship. He had shown that he was ready to take the next step to the NBA. Leaving Syracuse was sad. Anthony cried when he told fans he was not going to stay. But most of them understood. He belonged in the NBA with the best players in the world.

Carmelo Anthony

CHAPTER 3

PROFESSIONAL PLAYER

It had taken Carmelo Anthony a while to adjust to the New York winters. His next stop was not much warmer. The Denver Nuggets selected Anthony with the third pick in the 2003 NBA Draft. Denver is in Colorado. He would soon be playing in a city famous for getting a lot of snow.

Whether or not Anthony was ready for the Denver weather, the Denver basketball fans were ready for him. The Nuggets had been a really bad

Even as a rookie, Anthony quickly showed he belonged with the best players in the NBA.

team the year before. They had won only 17 games and lost 65. The fans could not wait to watch Anthony. They hoped he could help the Nuggets win more games.

That is exactly what he did. Anthony led the Nuggets to 43 wins that season. They lost only 39 games. The Nuggets even made the playoffs. Denver lost in the first round. Still, fans were thrilled by the improvement. It had been an amazing season compared to the previous one.

Many thought that Anthony should win the Rookie of the Year Award. After all, he helped his team win 26 more games than it had the year before. However, Anthony's friend LeBron James won the award.

Anthony got another new opportunity that summer. The US Olympic Team invited him to play in the 2004 Olympic Games. It was a huge honor. Anthony would get to travel to Athens, Greece, and play with the best basketball players in the world.

The Olympic Games did not turn out the way Anthony had hoped. NBA players had been playing in the Games since 1992. Team USA had won the gold medal in 1992, 1996, and 2000. But Anthony and his teammates only won the bronze medal.

The **2004 Olympic Games were not the positive experience**
Anthony, *right*, **had been hoping for.**

The US players were disappointed. Anthony was also upset about his playing time. He complained to his coach. Later, Anthony felt bad about the team's play and his complaining. He promised that he would return to the next Olympic Games in 2008. And he was determined to win a gold medal there.

Anthony soon turned his attention back to the Nuggets. They were even better during his second year. They improved their regular-season record to 49–33. But they still lost in the first round of the playoffs.

This pattern continued for the next several seasons. The Nuggets would win a lot of games during the regular season. Then they would lose in the first round of the playoffs. Fans started to be less impressed with both Anthony and his team.

Fans also were disappointed when Anthony got himself into trouble. The Nuggets were playing the New York Knicks in Madison Square Garden one night in 2006. Only one minute remained on the clock. Then a fight broke out. Anthony was involved. The NBA suspended him for 15 games.

The fight made many fans forget the nice thing Anthony had done just two days earlier. He had donated $1.5 million to

Every year, Anthony hosts a basketball tournament for kids in Baltimore. He calls the tournament H.O.O.D. (Holding Our Own Destiny) Movement. It's one of many ways Anthony tries to help the community. In 2005, he started his own foundation to assist kids and their families.

Through 2011, Anthony had never missed the NBA playoffs. However, success in the playoffs was harder to come by.

open a youth development center in Baltimore. The center was for poor children. It had basketball courts and classrooms.

Anthony had become one of the best players in the NBA. But he was finding fewer and fewer things to smile about.

Carmelo Anthony

CHAPTER 4

SMILING SOME MORE

Carmelo Anthony's fifth NBA season ended with another first-round loss in the playoffs. Anthony lived up to his promise to again play for Team USA at that summer's Olympic Games. Most of the best US players joined him. They were all determined to bring a gold medal back to the United States.

Anthony was one of the team's key players. In one game he made all 13 free throws he took.

Anthony smiles and salutes after helping Team USA win gold at the 2008 Olympic Games in Beijing, China.

Some people predicted Anthony would end up with the New York Knicks. Anthony married his longtime girlfriend LaLa Vasquez in 2010. NBA star Chris Paul gave a toast at their wedding. Paul suggested he and Anthony should join Amare Stoudemire on the Knicks.

That was an Olympic record. Anthony got the biggest prize later. Team USA beat Spain in the gold-medal game. Anthony scored 13 points in the victory. He smiled from ear to ear as he wore his gold medal.

There was even more reason to smile during his next NBA season. The Nuggets won 54 games that year. More importantly, they won their first-round playoff series. They won their second-round series too. The Nuggets finally lost in the conference finals. But it was a big step forward.

Anthony had a new reason to smile that September. He donated $3 million to Syracuse University. The money went toward building a new basketball practice facility.

The Nuggets came back strong in 2009–10. Anthony had perhaps his best game shortly after the All-Star break in February. The Nuggets were playing LeBron James's Cleveland

Anthony and his longtime girlfriend LaLa Vasquez married in 2010.

Cavaliers. Both Anthony and James scored 40 points. But it was Anthony who ended the game as the hero. He hit the game-winning basket with only two seconds left. However, the Nuggets again lost in the first round of the playoffs.

Anthony was only 19 years old when he joined the Nuggets. He led them to the playoffs in each of his seven seasons. But fans were getting anxious heading into his eighth season, in 2010–11. They worried the Nuggets would never win a title with their current squad.

People around the league began to wonder if Anthony would be traded. The Nuggets could get a lot in return for him. Anthony himself seemed open to the idea. Through 50 games, he averaged more than 25 points and almost eight rebounds per game for Denver. Then, on February 22, 2011, the Nuggets finally traded him. After almost eight seasons in Denver, Anthony was going home. He had been born in Brooklyn. He had gone to college in upstate New York. And now Carmelo Anthony was returning to New York City to play for the Knicks.

Basketball fans all over the state could not wait for Anthony to arrive. Some of them had cheered for Anthony at Syracuse. And they again cheered for him as he helped the Knicks reach

The Giving Back Fund named Anthony one of the 30 most charitable celebrities in 2010. The group cited his work with the Carmelo Anthony Foundation and other charities. In 2006, Anthony also created the Carmelo Anthony Youth Development Center in Baltimore.

Anthony and the Knicks reached the playoffs in 2010–11. The Knicks had missed the playoffs in the six previous seasons.

the playoffs for the first time in six seasons. New York lost in the first round. But it was just a start.

Anthony had already won a college national championship. He had even won an Olympic gold medal. Knicks fans hoped he could soon lead their team to the next big title: the NBA championship.

FUN FACTS AND QUOTES

- Carmelo Anthony has never lived anywhere near Texas. Still, his favorite college football team is the Texas Longhorns.

- As a kid, Anthony once sprained his toe while kicking a bowling ball. Luckily, this injury did not scare him away from bowling forever. While playing for the Nuggets he bowled at a charity event in Colorado.

- At 6-foot-8, Anthony is really tall. But he was not very big when he was growing up. The only things big about him were his feet. They were as big as most adults' feet when he was only 12 years old.

- Anthony's favorite food is seafood. But that was not always the case. According to an old neighborhood friend, one of Anthony's favorite foods as a kid was eggs, cheese, and ketchup.

- During Anthony's childhood, his mother was well known in the neighborhood. Many people even gave her a nickname: Miss Mary. Today, people still call her that. In 2008, Miss Mary helped feed 300 families on Thanksgiving day in Baltimore.

WEB LINKS

To learn more about Carmelo Anthony, visit ABDO Publishing Company online at **www.abdopublishing.com**. Web sites about Anthony are featured on our Book Links page. These links are routinely monitored and updated to provide the most current information available.

GLOSSARY

adjust
To get used to something.

anxious
Worried or afraid.

charitable
Giving. A charitable person gives money or assistance to people in need.

comeback
Winning a game after being down by a lot of points.

conference
In sports, a group of schools whose athletic teams play against each other each year.

experience
Having done something many times before.

opponent
Someone who is playing against you.

rebound
In basketball, to grab the ball after a missed shot.

recruited
Pursued by coaches who want an athlete to play for their schools.

rookie
A first-year player in the NBA.

varsity
The main team that represents a school in a given sport.

veteran
Someone with a lot of experience.

INDEX

FURTHER RESOURCES

Howell, Brian. *Denver Nuggets*. Edina, MN: ABDO Publishing Co., 2012.

Knobel, Andy. *New York Knicks*. Edina, MN: ABDO Publishing Co., 2012.

Ladewski, Paul. *Megastars*. New York: Scholastic, 2011.